DUKHNA NIGHTS!

DUKHNA NIGHTS!

A MEMOIR

Khalid Al Youssef

Translated from Arabic by
Abdulrahman Jones

DUKHNA NIGHTS!

Khalid Al Youssef

Published by Nomad Publishing in 2023
Email: info@nomad-publishing.com
www.nomad-publishing.com

ISBN 9781914325410

The Publishers would like
to thank the Harf Literary Agency

Printed in India by Imprint Press

Preface

It was a decade of time whose its days were present in every detail of my life, a decade that began with my birth, accompanied my growth, formed my memories, and became part of me. It was a decade of murky intimacy, a necklace that crystallized around me and took up a place in the pages that recorded my writings, so much so that from time to time, I sang the praises of its beauty.

Later in life, certain realities brought me back to that decade, and although I felt no conscious intent to so, it was my own affection for that time which accelerated the process. I went back to it with love, a passionate and nostalgic conversation that drew me back into its alleys, walls, houses, patios, and trees; back among familiar faces, sounds, words, and birds; back to the memory of abandoned names, terms, and slang.

That decade fell between the years of 1960 CE (1380 AH) and 1970 CE (1390 AH), and its depths inspire my writing. That period of time witnessed the innocence of childhood, but also fear and caution in the face of the unknown, as well as astonishment at how rapidly even small changes can transform a life. In the present writings inspired by that time, I have tried to draw the characters' features with all the differences that made them unique. I trust the reader also will find herein the rich legacies of beautiful customs and traditions, all scented with honesty and loyalty.

Dozens of friends and family members have unanimously agreed that this decade implanted fond memories in them, making it a time that deserved a book of its own. I wrote for them, for others who lived in this decade – and before it – and for those who will love those days forever.

These are the tales of Dukhna nights, which represented

an indelible aspect of our lives and were part of the transfor-
mations then taking place in all regions of the Kingdom of
Saudi Arabia. These were the days I lived through and during
which I witnessed the rapid development of my country,
symbolised by its capital, the city of Riyadh. These memories
depict how it was and how it changed, thanks to God, and
how it became a modern city, racing against time to become
one of the finest cities in the world.

July 3, 2021 CE

(23 Dhu al-Qadah 1442 AH)

Chapter 1

I do not remember the exact time when I started to become aware of my surroundings, and nor can I remember the age I was when I first realised some of the key features of my life. What I do remember very clearly, however, is the mud house in which I was born and where my life began.

It was a two-storey house with a big wooden door made from the trunk of a palm tree that had died dozens of years earlier. The carpenter had cut the round trunk into solid rectangular sections, each one over two metres long, which were then joined by three cross-pieces made from a tamarisk tree to form a semi-square door about two and a half metres tall and approximately the same width. The long wooden latch used to secure the door was a mechanical marvel, something of which the local industry in Najd was proud.

As for the house itself, when you first walked inside, you found yourself in a wide corridor with a roofed space leading to the rest of the structure. It could have served as a modern lounge but was in the style of that time.

On the first floor to the left, there was a small diwaniya, no bigger than fifteen square metres, which we used as a winter room because it had a fireplace. In the middle of the house was an open-roofed hall from which you could see the sky. Then there was a modest open kitchen attached to the hall. Actually, the word "kitchen" is something of an exaggeration. There were two kerosene stoves called kolas, a shelf for four pots of varied sizes, and another shelf for the tea and coffee pots. There also was a drawer for the tea and coffee cups and another for the cooking utensils. Annexed to this modest "kitchen" was a smaller room used for storage.

Opposite the storeroom was a corner that we called a 'glisten', used for washing and cleaning everything in the house – even for bathing. The water from the glisten was clean, and the drain ran into underground pipes that led across the alleyways and ended in the neighbourhood wells, from where it was used to irrigate the palm trees in the middle of the area.

Beside it was a small water tank made from metal; we called it a tanki and filled it with a special bottle which the saqqa brought to the house by prior arrangement, and for which we paid a fixed monthly fee. In winter, the water was kept in a round tank called a samour, which had an opening in the middle so that a fire could be started when we needed to heat the water.

To reach the upper floor, we climbed stairs that ran up the outer wall of the house. The first place you saw halfway up the stairs was the summer sitting room, called a roshen. It had open windows overlooking the roof, and opposite those windows were other windows overlooking the outside corridor, which was about 16 metres long.

The stairs led to the rooftop, where there were three more rooms: the first was neat and elegant with white walls, suitable for a newly married couple; the second and third were less elegant but also adequate.

In the corner, overlooking the outside corridor, was what is called a maqef, like a toilet; it had a small outside door from the exterior corridor. Once a month, a worker would come to empty all the waste and take it outside the city, where it was recycled as farm fertiliser.

The rooftop level also had a lower roof – this is where we kept our sheep and four goats, which provided milk. The other part of the roof – a little higher and on the northern side of the house – was designed as a sleeping area in summer.

Our house, which sat adjacent to several similar houses, was in a neighbourhood called Dukhna (meaning smoke) and known for an old well that formerly watered local orchards. It was in the middle of Riyadh, in an ancient area that used to be within the castle walls, just south of Al-Safa Square.

Next to us lived a family with a son, who was close to me in age, and two daughters, one younger than me and the other much older. On the northern side was a house where an old woman lived, and next to her was another house whose occupants, I recall, were related to a well-known family of high rank and status. They had a car and used to travel a lot.

The biggest house in the area was that of the Abusaleem family, one of the most important in Riyadh. Their work was related to the royal palaces, and their house looked very grand, with a huge main gate looking out in many directions. I still remember the night my father took me there after they had invited people from all over the neighbourhood. It was like a dream. I saw things I had never seen in our house – or anyone else's, for that matter.

Their house had a side entrance with a sekkah, which led to a staircase that went up to the roshen. This entrance took you up from near the main door into the alley, then onto a different staircase – ornate and perfectly symmetrical, with paint on everything around you. After that, you walked through a wide corridor lit by unusual lamps to the roshen.

As for the roshen itself, I had never seen anything so spacious and luxurious before; it could have been a hundred metres across. It was also the first time in my life that I had seen hanging chandeliers with white light-bulbs. The furnishings were a wonder to behold, each of the room's corners filled with woollen Roman carpets and a mix of modern furniture and traditional sofas and cushions,.

I also recall that there were several other large houses in this neighbourhood, such as Al-Sahabi's house, which was a part of the Al-Sheikh family – in addition to Sheikh Hamad bin Faris' house and Al-Tuwaijri's house.

We had lived in a smaller house before the one we were in at that time, and although I do not remember it well, my parents noted that it was "our old house" whenever we passed by. It was not far from the one I remember. In the heart of this neighbourhood was a well that I do not remember anyone pulling water from. Apparently it was deserted after 1963 CE (1383 AH), and facing it was a garden of small palm trees.

We had electric lighting, but only a single bulb in each room since the house's electric meters never exceeded five amps. I don't think that house had a single socket because we never had a device that needed electricity. If you wanted cold water, you had to use water from a water bag, or zir, and if you wanted to preserve meat, you had to put it in the arzalah, which was a basin or box made of wood or palm leaves. This would usually be suspended from the ceiling in the middle of the corridor, where the air flow was continuous most of the time.

We used the arzalah when we had extra meat, because the amount of meat usually lasted for one to three days – while the meat from Al-Adha had a special room in the upper floor, where it was cut into small pieces, salted, and spread on strong ropes. This type of meat was called kafar and lasted for a long time. Most homes prepared meat every day or every two days, in addition to fruits and vegetables. These were fresh daily meals, not refrigerated or preserved, especially since the prices at that point in time did not exceed 5 riyals per kilo.

Most vegetables came only during their respective seasons; there was no refrigeration or long-term preservation. Vegetables usually came directly from the farms to the markets, and from the markets to the houses, where they would be cooked immediately. The leftovers were kept in the arzalah, just like the meat, and covered with a moist burlap sheet.

As for the morning bread, we got it from the only bakery on Mohammed bin Abdel Wahhab Street, which was located at the southern end of the street, right before Dukhna Square. You had to be prepared for the morning queue, and to bring either a good towel or a canvas bag in which to wrap the bread and keep it warm.

This bakery served fresh beans as well, and often people came to purchase them with a tassa, which was a circular container with a lid, or a satel, which was more compact and sealed.

The bakery sold bread until just before the Isha prayer. Most families started getting ready to sleep shortly after eating dinner, so dinner time was known as Ishaween – the period between the Maghrib and Isha prayers.

Chapter 2

The previous chapter ended with a description of the bakery on Dukhna's Mohammed bin Abdel Wahhab Street, but at the earliest point where my memories begin, I had not yet gone there, at least not on my own. I needed to know more about the neighbourhood around me before I could find my way to the bakery and back. Thus far my knowledge of the surrounding area had come mostly from my father, and both he and my mother were very keen on my learning my way around. My mounting awareness, though, also gave me the first thing I needed to know, which was the answer to a question I often asked my mother: "Where is my father?"

I would see him one day and then he would be gone the next. This was how things were most of the time, until at some he was gone for days on end. That time, my grandfather told me that he would take me with him to visit my father at his second house. It was a surprise for me when I saw my father on his bed in this house, and I asked him, "Why are you here? Why don't you sleep with us at our house?"

He lifted one of his hands and pointed at the other, saying, "I'm injured. I broke my hand and, God willing, after it heals, I will come back to you!"

It was then that I learned for the first time that my father had two houses, and that his absences from us meant that he was at his second house, near Al-Muqaybara Market. I also discovered that I had siblings at this house; this was the first time I met them and got to know them a little.

My grandfather – my mother's father – Dawood bin Youssef had other things to do, and as he was close to us, he visited a lot. This gave me more opportunities to get to know some of the streets and alleyways in the area as I accompanied him from our home to his, where he lived with my grandmother and my uncle. Mostly, I did not take not much note of their home, except that it was in a modern block of flats; in other words, they were from a different class.

My father was also keen on taking me with him for some of his errands. This was how I got to know Al-Sidra Market, located to the north of our house. It was a market that sold a variety of daily necessities, but it was mostly for women because most of the shops carried things like women's fashion accessories, fabric for women's clothing, and kitchen utensils.

I also got acquainted with Al-Muqaybara, which was Riyadh's main market. In addition, I got to know the Sheikh Mohammed bin Ibrahim Mosque – a large mud mosque – whose muezzin was Sheikh bin Mufairij. But Al-Sidra Mosque at Al-Sidra Market was of modern construction, and it was the closest one to our house. That was why my father brought me there when he thought it was time for me to join a Holy Quran circle in the morning in order to learn to read and write. These teachings began with the Baghdadi rule of vowels,

which taught us how to pronounce letters in various ways –
and was one of the most important phases of my life. Our tiny
children's voices rose and fell and echoed as we practiced, like
a sweet, beautiful, and incomparable melody. We followed
this rule for all letters, which was useful in developing our
knowledge linguistically, as well as in writing.

As for Mohammed bin Abdel Wahhab Street, which ran
from Al-Safat in the north to Dukhna Square in the south,
it was lined with a wide variety of shops but was famous
for men's tailors hailing from what was then South Yemen,
more precisely from Aden. They all adopted the same look
by not covering their heads, and they spoke a dialect that
differed from the people of North Yemen. Some of them
remained in contact with their country through the radio,
which sometimes played Yemeni music.

Across the street, there were a number of dark-skinned
barbers whom we referred to as the takarna. They were from
Africa. The street also had grocery shops, which sold cold

drinks and kept them in large containers called refrigerators – without electricity. These containers had ice cubes, and the drinks varied between juices and the only soft drinks: Pepsi and its kin!

The most famous shop on this street was owned by a tailor, Abu Zaid. He was a Saudi who had turned his place into a gathering point for a number of neighbourhood men in the morning and after the Maghrib prayer. He had distinctive tailoring styles and sold vests, caps, and underwear, among other things.

There were also repair shops for dawafeer, which was a type of modern cooking stove that worked with kerosene – much better than coal. You could also find shops that sold new bicycles, as well as shops that repaired old ones.

Then we would reach Dukhna Square, famous for its beautiful fountain located in the middle. Adjacent to it were extensive gardens, surrounded by huge ficus and eucalyptus trees. At one end of the square, there was also a place where you could fill tanks with fresh, pure water.

Naturally, the fountain had become the focus of people's attention. Lots of them were fascinated by it – especially after lights were added in the middle of the water. People were mesmerised every night, wondering at how the water became so colourful and beautiful. It often seemed like it was the only fountain in Riyadh.

The shops located south of the Governor's Palace specialised in sweets, biscuits, tea, coffee, other kinds of foods, and new cooking utensils. These shops were mostly owned by some brothers who had come to our country from the Hadramout region – the Hadramis, as we called them. Then, in the midst of all this, a large shop selling a new type of laundry detergent was opened: its name was Tide, and it announced free gifts for everyone who brought a certain number of boxes of detergent. The shop became the new place to go for many women, who were enticed by these gifts, which consisted of modern kitchenware. Little time passed before Tide detergent became the main type used in all families, and its utensils were the first choice in most of our homes.

The Hadrami brothers were our neighbours, and they had family relations with most of the neighbourhood. The most famous houses in our alley were the house of Ba Hattab, Ba Wareth, Ba Wazir, Balsharaf and Al-Amoudi.

On the other side was the house of Bin Jahlan. Some of them lived in apartments on the main street, and they had introduced some foods that the women in our neighbourhood were not familiar with, especially during Ramadan. These included luqaimat, Quaker Oats soup, and vermicelli. All the foods we knew were our usual ones, like marasee and masabeeb, and almost all soups and foods contained semolina.

The Hadramis followed a fixed schedule in which they met up for lunch every Friday. Most Hadramis do not live alone; they live with their wives and families, and we rarely saw a single person among them.

After these experiences, my circle of knowledge about what

surrounded me in Dukhna expanded, mainly by accompanying my mother on visits to relatives in other neighbourhoods. During that time, I got to know Al-Dahu, which was on the eastern side of Mohammed bin Abdel Wahhab Street. I also explored Sheikh Mohammed bin Ibrahim Street. Its alleyways and large houses were spacious, and my uncle lived there next to the khan, which was a strange and wondrous building. It seemed to me that it belonged to a large family.

Among all the relatives we visited, I noticed they had a son who had a distinguished appearance and a refined personality. I later learned that he worked in radio, but at the time, I did not know what radio was.

The western side of Al-Muqaybara was called Garage Daleel, or Al-Sarkiyah, and I was able to see it when we visited a number of relatives there.

When my brother Abdel Hamid, who was born immediately after me, grew a little older, he accompanied me everywhere. With him helping, it was easy for me to complete the house chores entrusted to me by my mother.

When my father saw that my memorisation skills were on the right track, he wanted me to join the Ibn Sinan School – which taught both Islam and some sciences – so that I could memorise more of the Holy Quran. The teacher there was Sheikh Mohammed bin Sinan, who was of Yemeni origin but had been granted Saudi citizenship.

The school was not modern; in fact, it was very old, and it was a Salafi school founded by Najd scholars. The most beautiful thing about this school was that it was right next to our house, in Al-Salim House, which it had rented out to be used as its headquarters. However, I only attended the Ibn Sinan School for one day because as soon as my older brother, Abdel Razzaq, found out, he took to me a health office which issued a medical report approving my enrolment in primary school. Thus it was that I was officially registered at the Omar bin Abdel Aziz Primary School in 1965 CE (1385 AH).

Chapter 3

I learned from my friends with whom I played every afternoon that there was a device that displayed moving pictures, and that we could watch it in the coffee shop near us. My little brother and I went together to the coffee shop, which was in a back alley off Mohammed bin Abdel Wahhab Street on the eastern side.

The coffee shop was frequented by several different types of people, of various ages and nationalities. Most of them sat with a hookah in hand, and in front of them was Abu Arbaa'tea. As for the children, we all just stood there in front of this strange and wondrous device, each of us in a state of astonishment.

We learned to say its name and found out when it would be on, so we visited every day. One day, our mother felt our absence when she did not hear our voices in the alleys around the house. When we returned for the Maghrib prayer, she grabbed each one of us by our ear and asked, "Where were you? Where did you go?"

I did not answer right away for fear of punishment, and of being deprived of this new form entertainment. But she put more pressure on me, and as the pain began to increase, I responded, "We were watching TV!"

"TV? What is that? Where? Who has it?" my mother replied.

My fear increased even more, so I told her, "On the street ... At the shops!"

But my brother added, "No, no. In the coffee shop!"

Her anger increased, so she hit us, telling us, "The radio has not entered our house, and you were going to a coffee shop with those who smoke and drink to see this?!"

My brother and I received a severe lashing, after which we wept for a long time.

After that, the news reached my father, who decided to take

us to the Holy Quran memorisation sessions at Al-Muraqib Mosque in the centre of Al-Muqaybara. These were held after the Asr prayer every day. He said he would take us there daily to make sure we attended.

One day, there was a discussion among my classmates about television and what was shown on it. One of them told us that the Al-Muqaybara coffee shop turned on the TV every day after the Asr prayer, which marked the beginning of the daily broadcast. Following this revelation, four of us decided to sneak out of the session, go to the nearby coffee shop to enjoy cartoons, and then go back to the mosque. The mutaween noticed our absence and we were punished – more than once, as it turned out, for we repeatedly escaped to the coffee shops.

Other times I went to our first soccer pitch – whose grounds had been levelled by the feet of the players themselves – to watch these young men and their great skill with my own eyes. The pitch was formed where houses had been demolished at the end of Mohammed bin Abdel Wahhab Street. The dust of the clay earth rose, shrouding the silhouettes of those playing and attending as if they were in a war or obscured by a dust storm. Some of them gave me half a riyal to hold their regular clothes until the end of the match.

As a result of this, a new punishment was given to me by my mother, who did not want me to go where strangers and those who were older than me gathered. She warned me that the punishment would be more severe if I kept up such behaviour.

Then my mother's newly married uncle came to live near our house. He was from Zulfi, my parents' home city, which I began to hear about from their conversations.

I learned from her uncle that, before his marriage, he had resided in Kuwait, and I learned that this was a country far from where we lived. However, most of the people of Zulfi visited and/or worked there. This was confirmed to me when my grandfather and my mother's uncles sat and talked a lot about it – as well as by my father, who used to talk about his brothers who lived there. I gathered that he also had been to Kuwait but was convinced to return to Saudi Arabia after the death of my uncle Saud in a traffic accident. The living conditions in Riyadh had also improved, and the country was beginning to change a lot.

My grandfather once gave me a new schoolbag with notebooks and pens in it. The covers of the notebooks bore the picture of Kuwait's ruler, which became the subject of questions and comments about me at school. Some of my classmates even started calling me "Kuwaiti"! I soon learned that my grandfather imported and sold some goods from Kuwait – especially those that didn't exist in Riyadh. I understood from various conversations that Kuwait was ahead of us in everything.

During one sweltering summer, my father decided with his cousin, my aunt's husband, to hire a private car that would take all of us, including my grandparents, to spend the summer in their hometown of Zulfi. I was happy with this first holiday to see this Zulfi that I had only heard about from their conversations. The car, belonging to one of our relatives, came on time. It was a Ford model we called "Blakash" and looked like a mini-bus.

We set off late in the afternoon, using the new streets of Riyadh. I heard from my grandfather and others older than me that one long street was called Al-Shumaisi Street. At its end on the western side of the city, we turned to the right, and this road turned north.

It was a long road passing by large palaces, and at the end of it, we turned left. We approached a large gate on the left of the road. They said this was Nasiriyah, and its gate was closed. I had no idea what Nasiriyah was!

Then the road bent north, and at its end we turned left, and I heard them say this was the road to Diriyah. It was a one-lane road. A short while later, we reached Salbukh; a small village that began with a gas station, crowded with people. Here, the asphalt road ended.

At the end of the day, the driver set off into the wilderness, relying on his experience and knowledge, the car turning right and left. Then, after a while, we stopped in the desert, and they announced the combined prayers for Maghrib and Isha. The women began to prepare coffee, tea, and food around a fire.

After that, we all ate our dinner, and then we continued on the desert road in total darkness. With the call for the Fajr prayer, we approached our destination, Zulfi. We descended to it on a very bumpy road that cut through the Tuwaiq Mountains. The town was not well-defined for me because of the poor lighting. The driver took us all to the home of our aunt, my grandfather's sister, whose husband was my grandmother's brother, who was my mother's uncle. We were welcomed in their small house as guests for an indefinite period.

I soon set off with my brother and my cousins to explore Zulfi, which we knew was composed of three main towns: Al-Balad, which was the base and was located in the middle; Alaqah, to the north; and Al-Uqda, to the south. The latter was pronounced "Azdah", but I didn't know why. Unlike other towns spread to the south and north, Zulfi was located between the mountains of Tuwaiq in the east and Al-Nafud in the west. As a result, it was confined to this low, flat land that was fertile for agriculture and suitable for settlement.

We visited many places and got to know many decent homes and families. The invitations and their dates varied, and our leader on these occasions was my grandfather– whom I saw welcomed and celebrated in all the houses he entered, both by men and by women. Some of them invited us to breakfast, which was usually early, and some of them invited us to lunch, which was immediately after the Dhuhr prayer. Others invited us to dinner, which was immediately after the Maghrib prayer. For me, the most important visit was to my aunt, whom I heard about from my father. She resided in Zulfi with her two brothers, who were then working in Kuwait.

We went to see the Erayrah, which consisted of palm trees and houses within the Tuwaiq Mountains, most of which belonged to my mother's maternal uncles. We also visited Al-Sieh, where my great-grandparents owned houses and palm gardens. We learned, too, that the region relies on the gorges and drains of the Tuwaiq Mountains for irrigation, and water is available most of the year from its wells.

We also visited the edge of the nearby Al-Nafud desert but did not enter it, for that was an adventure requiring specialised vehicles.

I had acquired a lot of information about my relatives, as I learned that they were a very large family, spread out in most of the houses located in the central town of Al-Balad. I saw that they were the same religiously.

Most of them were imams, preachers, or teachers – except for those who had gone to Kuwait, Dhahran, or Riyadh to work and brought change and renewal to their lives. They were classier and more elegant, and they had newer possessions than others. I heard that most of the houses were furnished and equipped with purchases made in Kuwait. I suspected that this Kuwait was next to Zulfi, because there was a lot of talk about it.

In one of the neighbourhoods, I saw houses built with stones, which were unlike anything else in this country. They called them "buildings", and they were the latest in construction because all the houses of Zulfi were constructed with mud.

Days passed without us realising it, and by the time our visit ended, more than two months had passed.

Chapter 4

U nexpectedly, we moved to my grandfather's house in an upscale neighbourhood north of Riyadh. It was called Al-Fouta, and it was new and beautiful. Our move was not voluntary, but was instead due to my mother's illness. She could no longer do her housework, and she hated the house itself.

My grandfather's house was also shared with my uncle from Al-Sham, who had got married a few years earlier. My brother and I were happy to stay with them for as long as possible because they had a Philips television which we could watch every day. Prior to this, we had watched only furtively when we were able to sneak away to a coffee shop. But with one in the house, we could sneak to it every afternoon, standing in front of it in trepidation, perhaps for a few minutes or sometimes what felt like an hour.

It was on a small table, and we watched from the beginning of the broadcast until the end, memorising its programmes. We became familiar with the Saudi broadcasters and began to imitate their voices and performances. I first got acquainted with Abd al-Basit Abd al-Samad – the majestic reciter of the Holy Quran – when I saw him on my grandparents' TV. I was obsessed with the sentence:

"Baba Ali welcomes you and we salute you, too!"

It was the children's programme that was dearest to our hearts, as well as some American films. We loved to watch foreigners. As for the Lebanese series, they were of a different nature because they presented history and personalities as they were, helping our imaginations to show us that which we read about.

The radio in my grandparents' meeting room was the size of a table. They listened to the morning programme and the beautiful morning songs by famous singers: Fadwa Obaid, Fahd Ballan, Talal Maddah, and Mohammed Abdo. My grandparents' personalities were very different from those of my father and my uncles; they were not embarrassed by the sound of songs.

My grandfather, who always wore the ghutra and a white robe, was different from my father. He had travelled to Al-Sham, Kuwait, and Al-Zubayr. He did not see anything wrong with anything that God has permitted.

As for my father, he was a sheikh and was called Mutawa, who only accompanies scholars and sheikhs, and sometimes fear of my father took over my mother when he would visit us at my grandfather's house. She would rush to cover the TV and turn off the radio, repeating fearfully, "He doesn't know. He must not see the TV."

But my grandmother did not care and would reply, "Don't worry, leave it to me and I'll explain to him. You don't expect to have a radio or a television in your house?"

My mother replied, "That would be the last thing to happen in our house, and you know it!"

"What would he do if he knew about the films that my son puts on?" my grandmother asked. "What would he say?"

My mother used to warn me and my brother not to speak in front of my father about anything, especially the films that my uncle would put on from time to time – usually on Friday nights. It was an arrangement that we only watched films.

My uncle would start to prepare the machine early on, bringing the circular tapes (reels) and then checking that everything was safe. Then, those who wanted to watch the films started to arrive. This show was held in the hall of their small house, whose doors opened to their majlis. The men – my grandfather, my uncle, his paternal uncle, my mother's cousin, and my uncle's wife's brother – would sit in the majlis, and the women would sit in the hall. We saw another life on that screen; that's why it was an unbeatable joy.

As the days passed and the school year began, we had to

go to our school, which was near our house in the Dukhna neighbourhood. But my mother still could not stay there when we went back, so we returned to my grandfather's house in the afternoon that same day. Thereafter, my brother and I made our way to class every morning on foot, getting from Al-Fouta to our school in Dukhna via Al-Swailem Street and Al-Safat, then retraced our steps in the afternoon.

My brother and I got to know many landmarks during this phase of change. We often visited Al-Fouta Park to play there. We also got to know the northern part of the Al-Fouta neighbourhood, where there was a big tank from which we got water in plastic containers.

On Fridays, we accompanied my grandfather to pray at a mosque in the middle of the square, where King Faisal prayed. Immediately after the prayer, people would stand at the mosque to greet him, watching and waving, and some people would shake his hand. He never left quickly, but rather gave everyone the opportunity to meet him, despite the guards around him.

I also frequented Al-Khazan Street, memorising its features from east to west. I travelled Al-Zahira Street even more because that was where my aunt and other relatives lived. I also got to know Al-Atayef Street, which branched off from Al-Khazan Street.

It became apparent to me that most of the residents of these streets' buildings were from Al-Sham, having settled in Riyadh after coming for work. Their presence began to change the local people and spread something new in their lives.

They opened decoration shops that contributed to the aesthetics of new homes. They opened shops carrying curtains and modern chairs, and I saw a number of tailoring shops where they made foreign suits that we had never seen before. As for restaurants, they now offered falafel, hommus, mutabal, and various salads. I also saw a number of restaurants specialising in Shami-style grilled meats. All of these were opening in the vicinity of Al-Khazan Street and the streets branching off from it.

What was remarkable to me was that women in the streets of northern Riyadh did not cover their faces, and they were of different nationalities. Some of them did not wear the aba like Saudi women, and even some of the Saudi women only covered their faces lightly.

The Shami people's children were our classmates in primary school, and I found that they had a big influence on us. They brought something like pancakes with them which they ate during the long recess, and which contained stuffings we did not know, such as thyme with eggs or cheese, or falafel with tahini. Then we started copying them and changing our foods from the ones we were used to.

Indeed, the first postage stamp that entered my pocket came from a Syrian classmate, who introduced me to this hobby and encouraged me, telling me, "You can get many stamps from different nationalities in Riyadh! Foreigners come from everywhere!" Indeed, I started searching and collecting until I grew attached to this hobby, which gave me a treasure that I had not expected.

Our long stay in my grandfather's house allowed my observations to expand to many things I hadn't seen before, which grew my knowledge and imagination early on. By that I mean television and cinema, which influenced what I became interested in later on. I found out about dozens of Egyptian actors and actresses, whose films I watched in those days. I've watched and listened to Umm Kulthum, Farid al-Atrash, Abdel Halim Hafez, and Sabah since I was a child. In fact, I was always listening to Abdel Halim's song Above the Thorns – I'm still in awe of its beauty, melody, lyrics, and overall performance. This was in addition to the unforgettable concerts and songs of Farid al-Atrash. As for Umm Kulthum, that's a whole other world entirely.

There was another different reality in my grandfather's house. It was the openness of his majlis to different guests, some from the family, some from outside the family. All of them enjoyed watching television, and most of them wore headbands on their heads. In some of their conversations, there were words that I did not understand. They stayed up listening to the songs of Umm Kulthum and Farid al-Atrash on Friday night, and I would see some of them go out to the wide alley to smoke away from the gathering. This different reality created many questions for me, and a comparison between my father and my grandfather.

They were from two different worlds, but I never got any answers.

As for what was around us in the Dukhna neighbourhood after these changes, my brother and I accompanied my father on Friday to pray at the Great Mosque in Al-Safa. What was amazing for us was our knowledge of what happened after Friday prayers in Al-Safa Square. There, during those days, it was established and proven that this was the permanent day of retribution, as not a single Friday passed without seeing the police in a circular area that changed in size, smaller or larger according to what would be implemented within it.

We saw the floggings, which happened almost every week.

We saw the executions – by sword or by shooting – as legal punishment of murderous offenders.

We saw the hands of thieves cut off, including one of the students of our school, who had been expelled after his multiple crimes. He became a wanted fugitive, stealing, looting, and committing assault, one of the rejected people in the neighbourhood and in society, and it was a shock to us when we saw him without a hand!

There was also a punishment that was carried out which I did not see, but only heard of: the stoning of an adulteress. I did not know what that word meant then, but it had become the general talk of the town.

We moved from our house near Omar bin Abdel Aziz Primary School after my mother could not bear to return to our favourite home. We moved to a house adjacent to her uncle's and my cousin's houses in a closed alley. It was on the southern side of the Ibn Sinan Mosque.

After we had entered the alley and seen more than one house to dwell in, my mother refused to live there – for many reasons. She later told me that these houses were terrifyingly lonely, with ghosts in them; her hair would stand on end as soon as she entered them! There was one house that really frightened her, where she stayed only from morning until noon. Then she ran out of it and sat at the outer door waiting for my father to come. She said the reason was that the jinn wouldn't leave her alone while she was cleaning it, despite her reading the Holy Quran and consecutive supplications.

As for the house we ended up living in, it was my immediate family, my cousins, and the neighbours. We were originally six houses, but we spent most of our time together, eating, drinking, and playing in the alley, as well as wandering to new places.

Chapter 5

After we moved next to my mother's uncle's house, our collective family fun had no limits, while my father rested. In addition to that, we were next to the kindest family in Riyadh. It was a family consisting of an elderly woman with her daughters and granddaughters, who added more reassurance. But with all that, the house itself was extremely uncomfortable for several reasons. That was why we moved to another house adjacent to the Ibn Sinan Mosque, facing a wall of palm trees, called Nakhl al-Ward. Exactly opposite the door was a rakia which was fed by a plentiful well and almost never ran out of water.

In Riyadh, there were a large number of houtat, or al-huwaitat– this was how it was pronounced in our dialect – and it was said in ways like, "Hotat so-and-so," or "Howet so-and-so."

This area was where people came to perform their ablutions, and in its corner was a wall that isolated people from those who wanted to take a quick shower. As for the house we lived in, it was strange and interesting because it was very small, so there was only a small diwaniya on the ground floor to the right of the entrance.

On the left side, there was a staircase that took you to the upper floor, and under the stairs, there was a secluded bathroom. Then you entered the middle of the house, which was dark except for a light that came from above, from a square opening where the light descended into a small courtyard. It made strange sounds at times. That was why we spent most of our time on the upper floor, which was more open and comfortable. I always wondered why my father settled us in this strange, exciting house – despite daily complaints to him out of fear, panic, and unending loneliness.

Then, as if the lonely situation in this house were not

enough, my father took the initiative from time to time to allow those who wanted to perform their ablutions to enter our house, so they could finish their ablutions quickly, when there was a lack of water in the rakia! This upset my mother when she was shocked on one occasion by the presence of a number of men at the entrance of the house looking to perform their ablutions! When she talked to my father about this issue, he told her, "We only want the reward from God."

Sheikh Mohammed ibn Sinan would inspect the residents of the neighbourhood during prayers – especially the Fajr prayer. He would take out a piece of paper – in his capacity as the imam of the mosque – and call out their names. And they would answer, "Present."

If they did not answer, a group from the congregation went with him to visit this person who had missed the Fajr prayer. If everyone verified that he was healthy, they threatened him with punishment. This happened with all those who failed to attend the Fajr prayer.

Sheikh ibn Sinan was a leading religious figure, one of the first to open a school to teach people how to memorise the Holy Quran in Riyadh. His pale skin was usually blood-red, and I saw everyone in the mosque greet him with respect and reverence. I was the first of the children to greet him, which is how my father taught me to deal with others.

One day, a neighbour who was close to my age told me, "I want you to come with me to visit my mother."

I asked, "Your mother? Where is she?"

He replied, "In Badiaa!"

I asked him where Badiaa was, and he replied, "Close to Riyadh, on Al-Shumaisi Street."

I went to my mother to inform her of his wish, and she agreed after issuing warnings. I left with him and we got into a taxi. It took us along Al-Shumaisi Street, heading west to where it ended, then we continued west between new palaces, amid scattered spaces. The wide street began to bend south towards Wadi Hanifa, and we were in front of mud houses and new buildings scattered among them, and my neighbour said to the driver, "Wait here, and we'll come back with you after a while."

After he knocked on an ordinary door and called out, his mother answered him. She opened the door and greeted him, and he kissed her head and greeted her. She recognised me as soon as she saw me and asked me about my mother. I went out the door to wait for him after I left him with his mother. Not long after, he came out to me, happily carrying a bag of gifts from her. Then I asked him, "Why did your mother leave your house?"

He was silent for a while and then answered, "My mother got married to a new man!"

What I saw in our neighbourhood was that most of its residents were from Riyadh itself. As for those who came from other villages and towns, they were called by the name of their place of origin. My mother often sent me with special things and said to me, "Give this to Latifa, of Sudair," or, "Give this to Jamila al-Asiriya," or "Give this to Fatima Al-Jizania"!

This addition to the name was the imprint of a time and place, and a guide to knowing instantly which house to bring something to. The non-Riyadhis were not very numerous in our Dukhna neighbourhood.

Not long after, we moved to a house next to our old one. It was on the north side, and it was the newest, prettiest, and coolest of all. The entrance to this house did not face the sun, due to the presence of a mujaabbab between the houses in a wide alley.

The previous family had looked after it well, and it was spacious and luminous, with an open courtyard. The entrance was separated by a wall in the centre of the house, and to the right of its mujaabbab in the corridor was a wide diwaniya. To the left of the entrance, there was a staircase that took you to the roshen. It was spacious and large as well, and it had a small room, and then there was the roof. There it had two beautiful rooms, divided by separating walls.

As for the kitchen, it was separate, with a private entrance and pantry, and it had a private exit to the sheep yard. This house also had been whitewashed with pure white plaster, with Najdi Arabic embellishments.

In this house, I had my own room, which was within the roshen. While in it, I was able, for the first time, to save money to buy a small wardrobe containing my private things, and I was even able to make a desk for myself. After that, I bought a special chair for it.

Along my wanderings, I discovered a bookshop located south of Al-Safa, and I would go there to buy story books from time to time. I found they had an album for stamps. My first albums were stored in my cupboard after I became a greedy and constant stamp collector.

Then I found an offer in the studio next to the library: a camera with film for 7 riyals and a film developing fee of 3 riyals! It was here that I first entered the world of photography and began to learn the art of it, all of the angles and how to create real time images.

During this time, the markets around us – to the north, the Sidra Market, and to the west, Al-Muqaybara, Riyadh's main market for everything – began to expand. Al-Muqaybara got bigger, and old houses that were in the way of its expansion were demolished. The whole city of Riyadh also grew every day, and in every direction. The streets widened and extended their lines everywhere. The houses in the Dukhna neighbourhood started getting abandoned – except for those inhabited by expatriates. As for the original people of Riyadh, most of them left for the newer neighbourhoods – some of them on the outskirts of the city.

One day, my father took me with him to his evening work, which was in the Al-Malaz neighbourhood, a significant distance from Dukhna. To reach it, we had to ride shared taxis to Al-Batha, and each passenger paid a quarter of a riyal. At the end of Al-Batha Street, another car went to Al-Malaz for the same price.

When we passed by one new neighbourhood – a complex

of new one-storey concrete houses – my father said to me, "God willing, we will live here. I have booked two houses for you and your brothers, and the second house has a private house of its own."

All the streets we passed through were nice and wide, adorned with green trees and palms. When we arrived at his work, he said, "You look around the streets and shops, but take care so that you don't wander off and get lost."

It was early afternoon. I saw that most of the businesses were modern restaurants. Along with the presence of traditional restaurants, there were also shops specialising in modern clothes. Most visitors to these shops were foreigners, and I glanced at the garden we passed through from afar, and then went there. I spent some time there, watching the foreign women and children who visited it, and I remembered what I used to see in Al-Fouta Park.

In the evening, after our return, I told my mother and brothers what my father had told me, and she replied to me,

"It has been a long time since your father promised us that we would leave the Dukhna house and move to a new one. May he be able to save the money needed so we can leave these mud houses."

My parents had an orphan cousin who had been raised in Riyadh. After he migrated from Zulfi to work for upper-class families as a driver, one of his employers had put him in charge of many other jobs. He frequented my grandfather's house, as the latter was his uncle, and he always visited us and most of his other cousins too.

In other words, he was always at our majlis gatherings, and everyone loved him for his good companionship, the gentleness of his speech, and the elegance of his attire. He used cologne to hide the smell of smoke. He once presented my mother with a new radio as a gift for us, telling her, "Ahmed should not know that I am the one who brought it to you."

We often enjoyed his company in his car. He took us to a lot of new places, and this was how I heard him convince my father and my cousin, who lived with us in Dukhna, that moving to the new neighbourhood in Al-Malaz was the next step.

Chapter 6

People in our neighbourhood had one heart, and in that one heart, I saw that they lived in adjacent houses and were attached to each other – as were their feelings and souls. If anyone had a problem, everyone went to help them and stay with them through thick and thin.

I saw how tasks were distributed to the neighbours for the marriage of Latifa's orphan son, as if he was their only son, too. I saw how the men in the neighbourhood collected cash, headed by the imam. As for the women, they took charge of preparing everything for the wedding night. The groom's mother was not exhausted at this wedding, except from worrying about the wedding itself. This was their way in all their affairs.

In cases of damage occurring from heavy rains, which was usually the case every year, people's houses were opened to their affected neighbours. The houses would be rearranged in order for the affected neighbours to stay and be safe; men would stay together in one house, and the women with each other in another, until what was destroyed or collapsed in the affected house had been repaired. They also helped each other to restore and rebuild the houses in question.

I often saw the rebuilding of mud houses with square stones to help strengthen their foundations and provide protection from rain – especially since the mud houses were intertwined with each other, as though they were one house. The rain came in many ways and caused different kinds of events, which I heard from my parents and others in Dukhna, and in many other locations.

Although people were usually happy when it rained, sometimes it exceeded normal limits, causing tragedies and sorrows because most of our homes were on built on slopes that acted as runways for the rain. The mud houses were also weak – no matter how good their construction was.

The nature trips we took in the spring were also collective. My household and our car-owning neighbours often went out into the wilds around Riyadh – or we would go with a group of relatives out to a meadow adorned with spring blooms for days on end.

Among these trips was one to the lands of Dirab, located west of Riyadh, towards Makkah Al-Mukarramah Road. We stayed a whole week in the hinterland, and the land was blooming with more than a dozen types and colours of flowers and herbs. We would return to each of our schools in the neighbourhood in the morning, then we would all go back in the afternoon. Every day, as soon as the evening came, we would have new guests to enjoy the spring land with and to stay up with our family and have unforgettable nights.

On Salbukh Road – one of the main road leading north from the city of Riyadh – we went on even more interesting and beautiful trips. What was strange about that was that sometimes a taxi driver we did not know would join in the event.

On one such occasion, either my father or one of the other participants in the trip negotiated the fare with this driver, but after sitting with us, drinking, eating, and enjoying the journey like us, he forgot about the fare and said, "After everything you've given me, you want to give me money? I'm happy with what you've given me."

On another one of those excursions, a taxi owner accompanied us, as usual, and he was treated just like the others before him, but this man said to my father, "I will not take anything if you can promise me that I will be with you next week, if you want to go on another trip!"

After that, he was there every Thursday morning. He accompanied us on many trips, and to most of the gardens in the Riyadh region. That went on until he married one of the neighbourhood women who always accompanied us.

The first few non-Saudi families to live in our

neighbourhood were Pakistani. There was an acquaintance and a closeness between us and them, and they learned the Holy Quran, which was the first mediator between us and them, especially among the women. They were trying to learn about our customs and traditions, including wearing the Saudi abaya.

It was not long before these families became fully integrated into Saudi life.

The men were engaged in carpentry, and the women in embroidery, knitting, and tailoring. The most beautiful things I saw were their jewellery boxes, made with great precision, and with amazing shapes, sizes, and colours. As for food, they periodically shared some of their traditional fare with the neighbours, including Pakistani sweets, breads, and other dishes.

At quiet, still times, the music emanating from their houses was alien to us. It was their own music, which had a sweet flow and made them happy. On holidays, they danced to it, but they did not exaggerate the volume while listening to it, especially during the quiet times, for they did not want to anger the neighbours by violating local customs and traditions. They were loved by all.

However, one day something happened, and they just disappeared! One morning, we were awakened by shouting, arguing, and fighting among the men, representing four families. The fight escalated until knives and machetes were used; blood flowed among them, and the police were called. Every one of them – young and old, men and women – was removed from the neighbourhood. No one knows the reason for that battle, but after it, those families disappeared from Dukhna.

Around this time, I remember being given a tricycle, although I cannot recall what the occasion was. I also remember that it was never completely mine. As soon as my mother allowed me to take it out of the house, I rode up and down the alley on it. Other children heard the sound of its little wheels and followed me, cheering me on.

Everyone wanted to ride it, so they all courted me. I gave

opportunities to everyone, and that continued daily until my mother got tired of me and my dirty clothes, since I was spending most of my days wandering in the alleys. She decided I would not go out until afternoon, and so she put my trike in one of the rooms and locked it.

I noticed that the girls were the ones who courted her the most to take out the bike, so they could play with it. With all this persuasion, she allowed it out one day and refused the next, until a day of separation came. This was the day when the most boys and girls played with it, and my trike got smashed into bits and pieces. Then my mother said, "Praise be to God. Now we can get some peace from it!"

A few years later, I bought a bigger, two-wheeled bicycle, learned again quickly, and got just as good as before. Boys hesitated to use it, and we were at an age where girls were not allowed to play with bicycles – nor could they ride them!

But this bike almost caused me to permanently injure myself. Its triangular seat had a pointed edge that tore through clothes and hit my private parts! I fell to the ground in unbearable pain and, given that we did not have a doctor or a health centre, traditional medicine was the only thing available to us, so my mother used a mixture of herbs until the deep wound healed. By the grace of God, I recovered in time for a trip we took soon thereafter, and the bike problem was left for another day.

Daytime in our alleys was vibrant, as there was the noise of people going to the markets near Dukhna, and the hustle and bustle of those returning at sunset.

During the day, you saw the carts, pulled by donkeys, and the voices calling, "Coal ... Coal! Kerosene ... Kerosene! Faragna ... Faragna!"

Demand for coal usually increased in the winter, while kerosene was in demand most of the year. The faragna was a person who sold women's fabrics and ready-made clothes – or any women's items – after arriving in Riyadh from somewhere else. Usually, he did not start his work until afternoon and evening. He would keep his goods in a bag, a roll of large cloth on his head or behind his back.

The naughty boys would chase him until this roll fell to the ground and scattered its contents at his feet. They would laugh and take as much of it as they could. As for the dallalah, she was in our neighbourhood as well. She was a woman who sold everything related to women and children or practiced folk medicine. This was why she had different types of herbs from which medicines were extracted.

One of the peculiarities during the day in Dukhna was that you heard the voice of the Quran reciter Mohammed Rifaat on Friday morning from the open shops on the main street. On most days of the week, with the approach of the Asr prayer, you heard the voice of Abdullah Khayyat. As for Adenic songs, I used to enjoy them a lot, and Yemeni melodies in general, which were broadcast by the radio in Aden. I heard these in the sewing shops in Mohammed bin Abdel Wahhab Street. There was one song that was immortalised in my memory, which visited me from time to time in melody and performance. It was my favourite:

"Coincidentally, we met on the coast.

Coincidence in which passion tied two hearts.

I heard moaning on the waves, sighing when my heart touched you.

And the eye calls on eyes; the sea, the sand, and the beloved full moon

Witness the passion and friendship between the two of us."

Chapter 7

When darkness fell on Dukhna's alleys, with it came stillness, calmness, loneliness, and fear from the blackness of the walls and houses, as well as the sound of trees and palms rustling against the walls between the houses. After an already noisy day, people returned from the markets surrounding the neighbourhood from all sides, men, women, and children, each one carrying the harvest of their daily toil. Then came the sunset, bringing them back to their shelters, and the journey of the night began.

Dukhna's narrow alleys were special during the day, as they were covered by mujaabeeb that were close to each other, providing shade that reduced the flames of the sun in summer, and the cold of winter when outside the durability and solidarity of homes. However, due to the scarcity of lighting these added to the darkness of the night and drew ghosts along the mud walls. I never went out on my own for fear of these ghosts, for there was one of these above the walls of our house.

Above the Warrad wall, there was a long mujaabbab between the mosque and the house where the students resided. As for the alleyways that led me to my cousins' house, most of them were connected by mujaabeeb, too, and I always went with my younger brother.

In my cousins' house we had beautiful nights if we wanted to spend the night with them. We would all stand around their little TV. If it was winter, we'd be in their diwaniya, where men, women, and children gathered. Us, them, and the neighbours.

We were all following and fascinated by the evening series that drew us in, or by a musical evening with Umm Kulthum, which adults were happy with – as well as the evenings of Farid al-Atrash, Faiza, Shadia, and Abdel Halim Hafez. But the funny moment was when you saw that most of the attendees in the diwaniya had fallen asleep, so you could hear music and rapture mix with the sounds of snoring. These snores came especially from hardworking women who hadn't slept since early morning – but couldn't miss the group sessions among the neighbours.

As for the summer, everyone prepared the venue for the evening after sunset. It usually took place on the roof of their house, which was not large. Despite this, we had entertaining and unforgettable evenings, and it was normal for dinner to be served shortly after the Maghrib prayer; then, after the Isha prayer, the session began with their television and everyone was calm, watching and contemplating.

One day, I heard my mother's uncle tell her what he had seen one night after he left. At about four o'clock sunset time (that is, half-nine at night), he said, "You know, I do not walk at night unless I have a torch, so that I can see my way, since our alley is dark. After I entered my alley, I saw something moving from afar, all black. I prayed and sought refuge from Satan. I called out, 'Are you a human or a jinn?' I raised my voice in the name of God. The next thing I saw was a man and woman fleeing, the woman only covered in her black aba."

My mother laughed at him, and at the way he spoke, and asked him to be silent and hush up.

My mother's uncle's house was located in a closed alley, hidden from outside eyes. Once, on one of the long winter nights, he had found a sleeping woman, wrapped in a light blanket. She was shivering from the cold, and he decided to put an electric lamp over the door of his house. However, a few days later he was surprised by the absence of the lamp, and he found its broken remains on the ground.

There was a lute player in our neighbourhood, and his sorrows only moved after the first third of the night, and his playing flowed between the houses, infiltrating them with beautiful, melodious tones. Emotions moved us at times to accompany the playing in many words and songs, and everyone was used to his performances. He was the son of a well-known family, and he had a spacious room next to his family's house, a location for his evenings and fun, and since he did not disturb anyone, everyone was satisfied with him and his playing.

However, what disturbed the neighbours one dark night was that one young man came to enjoy the music session as usual, except for what happened after he started listening to the singing: he took out a small bottle from his pocket, and started drinking without the audience knowing. After a while, he started to get drunk, and he began to act and move abnormally. Then he went on to harass those present, and spoiled their evening. The evening turned into a fight, and the news reached his family and neighbours, which coincided with the night guards' passing. So they grabbed all of them and took them to the police station. After that, the beautiful nights of mirth were spoiled, and the sessions were cancelled.

After that, we no longer saw him during the day, carrying the lute on his way back and forth. We did not see the door of the room open; it remained closed for a long time. Rumours began to circulate about the reasons for his absence, and all of them agreed that he had some kind of problem, and the neighbourhood lost a singer who would have gone on to do great things and achieve great fame.

There was also a single woman who lived among our homes in a small house, which had a wide courtyard, surrounded by four rooms. This woman worked collecting cartons and her livelihood came from what she could restore to life after selling them at Al-Muqaybara Market.

One night, a strange smell emanated from her house, which raised questions among her neighbours, especially the women. As soon as they saw her in the morning, they flocked to her to ask about the smell from the evening before. She tried to avoid answering them, saying she would be late to the market, but they insisted, demanding an immediate answer. They even entered her house, and, to their surprise, they found a hookah in the courtyard – and traces of jarak before their eyes!

She tried to apologise, said that she wouldn't do it again, and asked that they cover for her. The incident ended after she promised to fill her house with incense, instead of the disgusting smell of hookah, and that she would not go back to doing such questionable acts.

After a few days, the smell of incense was thick among the walls of the houses, and it was an indication for the women that their single neighbour was having an evening party. This situation repeated itself at the end of every week, until one night, just before dawn, a police car and men from the morals commission came. With them was a man who, speaking in a low voice, said, "This was her house, and I'm sure you will find men there."

After a quick knock on the door, the woman opened, and the police raided the house. After searching all over, they found three men with her, not only one! Two of them were drunk, and the third cried, "You exposed us ... You exposed us, may God expose you!"

All the residents of the neighbourhood were dumbfounded. The shock on their faces was caused by a woman who had won everyone's trust, but her sun shone with shame on a new, dark day.

As for my peers, each one of them had different nights with their respective families, except for one of them, whom I used to see from time to time.

At sunset, he frequented the house of Said, one of the pigeon sellers in the southern part of Al-Muqaybara Market. We noticed him while we played together in the wide alley, when the pigeons started circling above our heads, flapping their wings individually and collectively. We saw them fluttering in the sky, exciting their lovers, attracting them. Then my friend said, "Who would like to go with me to Said's so we can watch the pigeons?"

But everyone's answer was, "Why do you want to do that? By God, if your father knew that he would slaughter you!"

He paid little heed to warnings and intimidation, so he went to see them from time to time.

One day, some of us were sitting in our playground just after the Maghrib prayer and we saw our friend walking, but he was crying, and his steps were unnatural. We ran and gathered around him, urging him to speak. We wanted him to tell us what happened, to quench our curiosity! But he did not speak. Then he got to his house and entered. A few minutes later, he came out with his father and his brothers, all of them chanting, "Said ... Said ... May God make you unhappy! Death is coming to you, Said!"

They went to Said's house, all of them standing there waiting for him, and as soon as he opened his door, hands grabbed him and pulled him out. Every one of them hit him on the side until his body shape was distorted. He tried to get rid of them and hit them back, but all the men of the neighbourhood were standing in the narrow alley.

One of the men went to the police to tell them what he had done, and what was happening at his house. The uproar was still going on when the police arrived, so he was arrested, and we never saw him again. This is what I heard my mother tell one of the neighbours.

Our house near the Sidra Market witnessed many incidents. Among them was hearing the chaste women's cries for help after sunset, upon the return of men and women to their homes. They would call to anyone who could rescue them from pursuing men, crying repeatedly, "Help me, save me from this corrupt man!"

And so on. How many times we heard someone knocking hard on our door! If, when she approached the door, she heard moans of pain, my mother would call out, "Ahmed, Ahmed, come and see who's at the door!"

Her intent was to scare the man who was after the woman who needed my mother's help. She would say, "When I opened the door, I found her with her clothes torn after he assaulted her!"

This happened with a number of women. It was painful that this happened – sometimes even in the middle of the day – and it would often happen the same morning with more than one woman.

Chapter 8

The Al-Shuwayr calligrapher's shop was located in the southeastern corner of Dukhna Square. There was another calligrapher, Al-Smait, whose shop was located in the Al-Qari neighbourhood, along the street leading to Al-Wazir Street and Al-Batha Street. A third calligrapher's shop, the most recently opened, was located at the beginning of Al-Sabala Street near the western side of Al-Muqaybara Market. This was where the calligrapher Abu Saad worked.

These three calligraphers not only had calligraphy shops where they also sold paintings; for me they were also a school, which was a pleasure and a delight. I often left our house and went to Al-Shuwayr's shop and sat in front of it to watch his work as he prepared the iron plates, then held the wide brushes and wrote what was required in beautiful Arabic calligraphy on them.

On one occasion, he said to me, "Whose son are you? Where do you live?"

I answered him and told him who I was. Then he said to me, "Did you study calligraphy?"

I replied, "Yes," and he said, "Then try."

And so he gave me an opportunity in front of the people in the street, but only after he showed me the way to hold the broad pen, or the two pens together. I had a large paper in front of me, and I wrote what I knew. Then he said, "Nice. You are ready to learn. Keep writing and you'll see how you can become a better calligrapher than me!"

I found that the regular notebook I had was not enough, so I asked my father to buy me a big one, with stiffer paper that we called "card paper".

Until I got to know Abu Saad, one of the others calligraphers, what had intrigued me about him was that he was not only a calligrapher, but also a painter who created paintings of different sizes, shapes, and features. I went to see him a lot, standing in front of the small shop, examining his style, method, and production. I liked his drawing, in addition to that one line that stuck in my head, while dreaming of an upcoming artistic future.

There was a small library next to the studio under a large building overlooking Al-Safa, and I would go there from time to time and buy a story book from the Green Library series. My rival in this was also my first cheerleader, my neighbour, Fahd Al-Abdullah, who was also a classmate and a teacher. He was able to buy more stories than me, so he used to give me what he finished reading. He would even give me a small magazine called The Little Cub.

Then I learned that his older brother got it monthly with the Defence Magazine, as he worked for the Ministry of Defence, so I built up a collection of them.

Other times, we would go together to the institute

parties, which were at the Imam of Daua Scientific Institute in Dukhna Square. My mother was very reassured by our companionship. At the institute's concerts, I saw theatre for the first time in my life, and I also heard how poetry was recited in front of people, and I wished that these concerts would take place every day.

On other days, I experienced something different, as it reached us while we were in our neighbourhood. The sounds of military music were loud, so I joyfully rushed with my brother and some of my peers to Al-Safa Square, as we knew that it was there for a reason: this band and a military parade indicated that the king had arrived at the main palace. We did not know the reason; all that mattered to us was to enjoy the music of this diverse band, the various military shows, and the beautiful movements of the leader. After they returned along Al-Zahira Street, we accompanied them until the squad reached their destination, which was in a building opposite Al-Fouta Park.

The route that I sometimes took to go to the modern Riyadh Bakery, which sold the most beautiful types of bread, was not an ordinary route, because I went with my younger brother, Abdel Hamid. Other times my two cousins were with us, so there were usually four of us, crossing Dukhna Street from the north. We would turn right at Al-Thumairi Street towards the east, and then we would turn left towards the north on Al-Wazir Street, going all the way to the end of the street, where the bakery was located. On the way, I usually stopped by a library. It seemed to be a library that dealt with foreign books and periodicals, but I don't remember what it was called.

Then we all got to know the Riyadh Studio, which was in one of the back apartments on Al-Wazir Street, where I had my first photograph taken. The ghutra I was wearing in the photo was from the exhibits in the studio, not mine. Then this studio became a regular staple of mine, as most of my next photos were there. I even introduced my friends to it, and it was better than Abha's Studio, which was located under the court.

Sometimes our route led us back to the area that sold music records, via Al-Shumaisi Al-Jadeed Street, and often the whole afternoon passed, until the call to Maghrib prayer came, while we were watching and enjoying listening to songs in these shops.

The route could also lead us to the Municipal Garden, which was located between Al-Wazir Street in the west and Al-Batha Street in the east. After we discovered that it was more beautiful and wider than our little garden in Dukhna Square, we would spend a lot of our time playing there. But fear set in after the recurring presence of a strange person there, which stopped us from either sitting or even passing through it.!

At one point, I kept passing by the bookstores located in the Weekly Haraj, north of the Great Mosque. I enjoyed seeing books displayed on the floor, but I didn't understand most of the titles, and I rarely thought of buying a book from these shops because I thought they were for older men. That was until an opportunity came, and I dared to buy a book, on which was written: "Short Stories". Then I bought something else: the Kuwaiti magazine Al-Arabi. I started educating myself with a number of publications on a variety of subjects.

After my repeated visits to the National Book House on Al-Wazir Street, accompanied by my brother Abdel Mohsen, and seeing dozens of books on their shelves or otherwise on display, I developed the idea to form a library in my imagination, or to collect books that I loved.

Our visits and our overnight stays with my aunt showed me other things that we did not have in Dukhna. In particular, I noted two buildings on Al-Zahira Street; the first was Al-Nasr Club, and the second was Al-Hilal Club. We used to go to them to discover new things. Sports fans who followed football and other games went there. The activities at the clubs started after the afternoon prayer and went on until late at night.

At other times, we spent our time watching football, on a pitch to the east of Al-Fouta Park, and our fun was second to none, especially since the games were played by strong professional players. Some of them were among the prominent names in football stadiums, so when we saw them in front of us, we admired them and their extraordinary athletic prowess.

The biggest step in my life came when my grandmother, Lulwa Al-Abd Al-Rahman, kindly chose me from among her two daughters' children to accompany her on her trips to Zulfi, which allowed me to spend the most beautiful days with her. I carried the words I heard from my grandfather Daoud as a testament to my great status, "You see that you take my place, and you are the caretaker and the protector of your grandmother. Pay attention to her."

Whenever it was decided that I would go with my grandmother to Zulfi, we would sit next to the driver. We were usually with my cousin Ahmed bin Hamoud, and the real pleasure was when I saw the desert in front of me, extending as far as the eye could see. I saw the beauty of the horizon, the few trees, and some scattered herbs, particularly the rue that abounded in the land of Najd. The road paved with asphalt ended at the village of Salbukh, and the car took us up and down, passing between valleys and across undulating dunes of light or heavy sand.

The battle was to get out of it safely. If our trip was in winter, we had to deal with obstacles created or hidden by the rain, including flash floods and unseen obstacles. We would stop for long periods of time in order to avoid such dangers. But the rains also brought beauty to the desert, greening it with charming seasonal plants. This made me wish that the journey through the desert would not end. If our trip was in the summer, however, it often began after the Asr prayer, hoping to catch moderate weather since the nights of Najd were typically quiet and still, and a breeze would be a welcome refresher.

I accompanied my grandmother on a number of visits to her family in Zulfi, and each time my circle of acquaintances there, both male and female, expanded. I was most excited about the girls I played with. They liked my appearance, my clothes, and the way I talked, and when I told my grandmother that they appreciated me, she would reply, "You are a child of Riyadh, and everyone wants to play with you because you are as attentive as the children here, your clothes are white, and I bathe you every day and make you smell nice."

She did not accept that I bathed in water brought from open wells, but rather insisted that I bathe in pure, clear water intended for drinking. She told her brother once that "Khalid is dear to me, and I do not want him harmed by the red water."

It was known that most of the water used in Zulfi was rainwater.

This intimacy also brought me closer to my grandmother when we were in Riyadh. She would have me over to stay with her for many nights, and I would be very happy to serve her, carry out her requests, and accompany her on her many visits.

Chapter 9

Not a day passed without arms going back and forth; Al-Muqaybara started to turn on itself.

Due to the speed of its expansion, everything was mixed up. Everyone bought and sold, and everyone had stalls and places where they sold various things. Men and women, young and old, natives of the country and a few new arrivals: they all came for its wide fame, which quickly spread everywhere and attracted all those who wished to trade, from the villages, the desert, and other cities. Therefore, anyone who did not own a place, or could not afford to sleep on the land, would use a three-wheeled cart to ply their wares. They would stop every so often to call out what it contained, so you could hear the disparate products lists being announced from the beginning of Al-Muqaybara Street in the north, all the way to where it ended in the south.

These vehicles had everything you could – or couldn't – imagine! Like a popular mobile pharmacy. Or a bakery that sold different kinds of bread – especially one that was new to our Najd life, which was called shreek. There was even a baby-clothes cart, and one with toys and other gifts for children! It was the strangest of things. You would find women selling all kinds of snacks – even plant seeds – in a special cart! They all competed to see who could sell the most.

Al-Muqaybara, which occupied the centre of Riyadh and was called Al-Dirah after it embraced other neighbourhoods (Al-Qinai, Al-Sharqiya and Al-Muaqiliyah), imposed its expansion on all the houses overlooking it. The whole area turned into shops for buying and selling, the houses overlapping with the scattered shops, as it reached the south to the start of Al-Sabala Street, north to Al-Shumaisi Street, and west to Al-Atayef Street – while to the east, it overlapped with other markets. With the speed of demolition, removal, change and renewal, it mixed with neighbouring markets, and the new name, Al-Dirah, took control of every place in central Riyadh.

We lived and saw the transformation in front of us every day, so I saw growth creeping into its roots. I saw that it grew faster than us humans, and I saw that its vast areas occupied all homes in order to increase sales by adding new display spaces and new merchandise.

It was no longer the Al-Muqaybara I knew, but a totally new place. I saw how Al-Muraqib Mosque remained alone in the middle of Al-Muqaybara, but I also saw the water-bearers carrying water skins on their backs, sprinkling water on the ground to keep down the dust blown onto it by the demolition of houses. Then, the water-carrier and his water carriage were replaced by a small water truck which the municipality had brought instead. They sprayed the ground with long hoses, and after days of watering the earth to control the dust, vendors would be racing to get their shares of space to make sure they had enough for their wares. Only two sections for vegetables and fruits were built in Al-Muqaybara, and they were on the western side of Al-Muraqib Mosque – to which a number of shops were attached, which specialised in selling other kinds of food and groceries.

In the north of Al-Muqaybara, I got acquainted with the first refrigerators thanks to large cars, which brought in freezers or coolers. They also sold imported fruits and meat there. In front of me was Al-Sharbatly's refrigerator, Al-Sudairi's refrigerator, and Al-Manjum's refrigerator.

On the western side of the section, there was Al-Zahrani's store, which specialised in fish, chicken, and other imported frozen goods. The people of Riyadh started buying eggs, chicken, fruits, and cheeses in all seasons. After opening imports from everywhere, here was Al-Muqaybara embracing all of these.

In the space between Al-Qaisariya and Al-Shumaisi's Old

Street, there was a landmark. It was the scale, and the parking lot for the daily freight cars that brought everything new: an instant auction ground. There, I saw buckets and bags carrying locusts, wild ghee, grouse, palm pollen, birds, and other products. This space also corresponded to a group of shops specialised in selling leather and salt. As for the eastern square opposite it, there were ice cars on the blazing summer days.

In the northeast of Al-Muqaybara, directly north of the Sidra Market, there were three elegant sections – or rather one section with three entrances.

The most famous place there, however, was in the southwest corner. This was Al-Mlouhi, a store for household utensils. It was famous not only among the people of Riyadh in general, but outside Riyadh, too. This corner became ubiquitous in people's conversations, and phrases such as "In front of Al-Mlouhi's shop," or "He waited for me at Al-Mlouhi's place" became regular parts of dialogue when describing a place or setting a date. This was especially true among women since they were the ones who most often went to and shopped at this shop.

Not a single day passed without an incident there, as it was where young men went looking for women – for flirtation, touching, and otherwise seeking to be close to them. Unlike what happened at the Sidra Market, which will be described below.

This section also featured the finest textile shops, as well as exchange shops, especially on the northern side.

Then came the beginning of Al-Suwailem Street, which separated two sections. The western side held a mix of shops offering various items, and most of its eastern side specialised in selling household utensils. The most famous of these stores was Al-Duraib: it was a traditional section and its roof was made of tin and wood.

This area was called Al-Hasawiya Market. You would enter it from the south, and you would see modern shoe stores which sold imported shoes, in which your feet would find a different level of comfort from the local shoes. One was called

Zubairiya, named for a leather shoe made by hand. Then, to your right and left, there were shops selling oud, incense, and oriental perfumes.

Among the most prominent of them was that of my uncle Nasser, who preceded others in importing saffron, and it was named after him: Saffron Abu Shaybah. I often visited to greet him and sit down with my dad.

Then, in the north of this section, there were shops that sold ready-made men's clothing, or what was required to be sewn into clothes, veils, caps and/or trousers. The people of Al-Ahsa became famous for this trade, and that was why the market was named after them.

From here, you'd head on ˋto Ushaiqer Market. It had a variety of goods, but stationery was taking over, and there were some shops that sold books and all kinds of stationery. On the western side of these overlapping markets, you could find another corridor, which had a market specialised in leather industries.

As for the corridor adjacent to it to the west, this was the low-lying Al-Jafra Market, to which you would descend, and that was why it was called Al-Jafra. It was a market for the wholesale of fabrics and food. In the street opposite the Great Mosque, watches had begun to spread, in addition to some other new devices, such as radios, televisions, and others.

The Sidra Market was a comprehensive market for both women and men, extending from west to east. In other words, it was facing the start of Al-Suwailem Street. On its sides, it had different shops, and its roof was like many others, made of tin and wood. Some fans and dim lamps were hung from it, and gold and silver shops gathered under it. Then the market extended and meandered to shops selling women's necessities and accessories. Women started buying these as a substitute for the gold that was too expensive for them, as well as different types of cosmetic products such as eyeliner, creams, cheap perfumes, women's fabrics and abas. At the end on the eastern side, there were household utensil stores. In the middle of this market was Al-Sidra Mosque.

I had heard that this market was a place for flirting and courting women, and that dates would take place in its narrow corridors. That was why there were a large number of mutawa, men of the morals commission, and their presence was continuous from morning to evening.

I always saw the commissioners' car and the police standing in the market square. Then the back would open, bringing out men who were masked with their ghutras, their hands cuffed. Someone would read from a paper, in which he explained what that person had done, and what the ruling against him was; then he was flogged in front of the people while he was standing, with either ten, fifteen, or twenty lashes – depending on his crime. Most of the crimes consisted of harassment of women, touching them, or attempting to do something even worse.

This was my tour of my beloved market, Al-Muqaybara, and the markets surrounding it. They were close to me because I visited them daily, either accompanied by one of my parents, or one of my peers, who enjoyed discovering these shops with me.

I never went to get something that my mother wanted without turning that task into a voyage of exploration. I would often receive a punishment and a threat of a greater one if I was late again! Yet still, I would continue to explore.

The south of the market witnessed the opening of the first Afghani tamees bakeries, more of which later spread into the market – especially in the south. Next to it was a café, with chairs spread over a wide area and a staircase reaching high off the ground, on which the television was placed – in addition to blinds that were offered to those who asked for them.

Baskets for the daily sale of imported fruits – which refrigerators allowed to be brought from everywhere – began to spread. As for the farms surrounding Riyadh, they only knew the beautiful yellow citron and buckthorn, which we called the "Hebrew". Then, a place was allocated for the sale of chickens and pigeons, and that area expanded rapidly because young people went there to acquire the latest types of pigeons.

Al-Muqaybara had a different atmosphere in Ramadan, and I learned about the Holy Month at an early age. I began to realise that when the month of Ramadan came, fasting was part of the home, the neighbourhood, and the people as a whole. There was no cooking, and therefore no smell of food in the house, in the morning or at noon, and my mother would tell us that we were in the month of Ramadan, and people didn't eat during the day.

My father would take me with him to the mosque on some nights of Ramadan to attend Isha and Tarawih prayers. Ready-made foods were spread out immediately after the noon prayer, including fried foods, especially luqaimat. Samosa was also sold at Al-Muqaybara.

Daytime at Al-Muqaybara Market was lively with traffic, and most of the markets around it were just the same. By contrast, the markets were deserted at night, with no sales, no people, and no movement.

Despite all of Dukhna's changes over that decade, that is the one thing that stayed the same:

Lively days and smoky nights.

Special Thanks

Standing beside me was my brother, Mr. Saleh bin Ibrahim Al-Hassan. He has my sincere thanks and gratitude

****

I also thank everyone who stood with me and provided me with information and pictures.

Acknowledgments

Special thanks and appreciation to my friend Mr. Saleh ibn Ibrahim Al-Hassan for his support and to all those who provided me with information and photos.